Happy Endings

EDNA McHUGH

HAPPY

ENDINGS

A BOOK OF DESSERTS

Illustrated by Murray Tinkelman

COLLIER BOOKS

NEW YORK, N.Y.

A Collier Books Original

First Edition 1962

Collier Books is a division of The Crowell-Collier
Publishing Company

Library of Congress Catalog Card Number: 62-12867

Introduction

MY MOTHER is a terrible cook. When I was a child, one of her great specialties was chocolate cornstarch pudding with lumps. I adored it. I've adored desserts ever since. But I've since learned that chocolate pudding shouldn't have lumps in it, and so I've taught myself to make chocolate pudding without lumps. I didn't learn overnight. For a long time *my* chocolate pudding had lumps. Perhaps this was an inherited characteristic. But I overcame it.

My first culinary efforts had a monotonously predictable ending: disaster. Once, at the very beginning, I made a dessert called Surprise Cupcakes: a small amount of batter dropped into the muffin tin; a spoonful of jam; and then more batter. The "surprise" should have been the jam in the middle. But I wasn't very familiar with stoves then, and so I placed the muffin tin under the broiler. Of course the cupcakes didn't bake. They ran all over the stove. But I did learn the difference between the oven and the broiler.

Even later on, when I was much more experienced and felt qualified to experiment, I had many results just as frightening. I once got the notion to make a cake with rivers of liquid chocolate running through it. I carefully placed cones of paper at intervals in the cake batter, and poured chocolate sauce in the cones. I wasn't quite sure how I was going to get the cones out of the finished cake, but I didn't have to. They caught on fire.

My experiments haven't always been restricted to desserts. Anything good to eat or drink fascinates me. Once I tried heating a popular soft drink, thinking I would hit on some marvelous hot drink to replace tea or coffee. I wouldn't recommend it. One of my best ideas (I thought) was making bourbon popsicles. I waited impatiently for hours for this new cocktail treat to be ready. But naturally the alcohol prevented the mixture from freezing (so I was later told), and another great idea fizzled. I've made peanut butter custard, licorice cookies, chocolate strudel, and other concoctions, many too nauseating to mention. My conscience bothers me terribly when it comes to wasted food. And so, on many occasions when I've been unable to press my experiments on unsuspecting friends, I've been sick.

Today I can invent a recipe and know pretty well how it's going to turn out. Not always; there are still some goofs. But almost always.

I don't recommend a steady diet of the richer recipes in the book. In the first place, you'll get too fat. I myself gained six pounds twice during the writing of it. I guess you'd say I really gained twelve pounds. I had to diet quite strenuously between testing recipes. But then there's no need for you to eat them as regularly as I did. I've done it for you. Of course rich desserts aren't really good for you; not good for the body, that is; but marvelous for the spirit. Some women go out and buy a new hat when they're feeling low. I eat a chocolate mousse. Some women become alcoholic at the end of a love affair. I eat a banana cake. Taken in moderation I don't think that eating desserts can do any harm, and you certainly ought to serve them to guests. The rest of the time eat fresh fruit.

People ask me where I get my recipes. The answer is, "Everywhere." Sometimes I think of a nice taste and texture and invent something that will satisfy that notion. Often I'll have a dessert in a restaurant or friend's home, and if it appeals to me and I'm able to get the recipe, I'll experiment with it—adding or subtracting, changing the method of preparation until it suits my taste exactly.

I collect recipes all the time. Some recipes I've tried to make haven't turned out at all, or turned out dreadfully. They were dreadful recipes, badly written. I don't think you'll have that trouble with the recipes in this book: seventy-one of my favorites. If you can follow a recipe at all you can make any of them. And if you love desserts, you'll love them all.

Not all these recipes are rich. For instance, there are some marvelous fruit concoctions. There's even a carrot cake that doesn't contain butter or flour. But they are all special. By special I don't necessarily mean epicurean, since one is a plain baked custard, for instance—but there's also a recipe for apricot pancakes that could top off the most elegant dinner.

Don't stint on ingredients. When I say "butter," I mean butter. When I say "chocolate," I mean chocolate. And when I say "heavy cream," I mean heavy cream. It makes a difference, so use the ingredients as listed to get the proper results. Most of the desserts can be frozen in advance or at least made the night before; there's no excuse for not serving something special for dessert when you have guests. There's no need to serve store-bought cake or, heaven forbid, instant pudding. At any rate, don't invite me if you do.

Have the proper baking utensils. You won't need very many. But remember that a cake that calls for baking in an 8-inch square pan and is baked in an enormous oblong pan just isn't going to turn out right. And don't blame me. It would be very nice if you had one of those marvelous fluted soufflé dishes in the 8½-inch size for most of the puddings and fruit desserts. Why not treat yourself to one?

After you've gone through the book (and it will take awhile; remember: not a rich dessert *every* night), try experimenting. If you feel that the maple mousse would suit you better with the addition of some chopped nuts, add them the next time you make it. But try the recipes my way the first time around. You owe me that. Remember those twelve pounds. I mean six.

Except in a few instances, I haven't stated the number of people each recipe will serve. This is because servings vary with individuals. Some people will take a bite and they've had it. Others (like me and my friends) can finish an entire chocolate soufflé on their own. You'll have to use some of your judgment, but on the average, I think you'll find that most of the puddings will serve about eight people and the cakes about twenty.

I must acknowledge the help I received from all of

my friends while compiling this book. They were extremely enthusiastic and encouraging. I could have done without some of the comments, including the one that runs, "It's good, but my mother used to make it better." (It probably had lumps when she made it, but they don't remember.) However, they were indeed a help when it came to disposing of the rejects, and there were many.

When I took cooking in grammar school our first instructions were, "Don apron and headband." That line always makes me laugh. I don't even wear an apron. I live on the ocean, and do most of my cooking in a bathing suit. When it turns cold in the winter, I switch to blue jeans. Obviously, what you wear is not important. However, other first instructions should always be followed, and these are: Read the recipe through. See that you have all the required ingredients, plus the necessary utensils and tools. Make note of approximately how long the dessert will take to make, and be sure you have sufficient time to see it through properly. Notice if any portion of it must be chilled, heated, melted, softened, or cooked in advance. Then get ready, get set, and go. Happy endings!

Malibu, California
1961

Contents

FRUIT DELIGHTS

GOOD AND HOT

LOVELY CAKES

LUSCIOUS FROSTINGS

SHEER DELIGHT

SOME MARVELOUS THINGS

"WHAT'S IN THIS CAKE?"

Happy Endings

Chocolate Heaven

CHOCOLATE BROWNIES

5 squares unsweetened chocolate
¼ pound butter
½ cup shortening
4 eggs
¼ teaspoon salt
2 cups sugar
3 teaspoons vanilla
1 cup sifted all-purpose flour

Set oven at 325. Grease 9″ square pan. Melt chocolate, butter and shortening together over hot water. Mix thoroughly, let cool slightly. Beat eggs with salt till light. Add sugar gradually and beat till creamy. Add chocolate mixture and vanilla. Fold in well. Add flour all at once. Beat till smooth. Bake for 50 minutes or till done. Toothpick should come out clean when testing, but texture should be soft and moist. Cut into small squares while hot.

I serve these practically every way but raw (which might be an idea). Put them in a bowl hot from the oven and top with ice cream. Crumble them and cover with sweetened, flavored whipped cream. Freeze them and serve them still frozen and chewy. Or just let them cool, if you can wait.

CHOCOLATE CAKE

CAKE

4 squares unsweetened chocolate
¼ pound butter
1 cup hot water
2 cups sifted cake flour
2 cups sugar
¼ teaspoon salt
1 cup sour cream
1 teaspoon vanilla
1½ teaspoons baking soda
2 eggs, beaten

FROSTING

4 squares unsweetened chocolate
7 tablespoons milk
3 cups sifted powdered sugar
pinch of salt
1 teaspoon rum flavoring
⅓ stick butter, melted
chocolate sprinkles

Set oven at 350. Grease a 13 x 9 x 2 oblong pan. Melt chocolate over hot water. Melt butter in hot water, bring to a boil. Mix melted chocolate into butter and water. Sift together flour, sugar, and salt. Pour chocolate mixture into flour mixture all at once and

blend well. Add sour cream, vanilla and baking soda
and mix well. Add eggs. Bake for 30 minutes or till
done. When cake is almost done, start making frosting:

Melt chocolate over hot water. Mix milk with powdered sugar. Add salt and rum flavoring. Add melted
chocolate and mix well. Add melted butter and beat
some more. Spread on cake while still warm. Cover
surface with sprinkles.

*There are chocolate cakes and chocolate cakes, but
this is it. It's moist (and stays that way) and chocolatey
and sheer heaven. . . . What more can I say?*

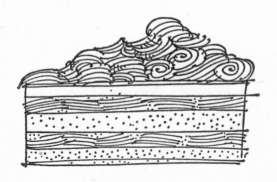

CHOCOLATE DESSERT SUPREME #1

1 pound sweet chocolate
1 teaspoon water
1 tablespoon flour
1 tablespoon sugar
¼ pound butter, softened
4 eggs, separated

Set oven at 425. Grease an 8″ spring-form pan. Melt chocolate with water over hot water. Remove from heat and stir in flour, sugar, and butter. Mix thoroughly. Beat egg yolks well, then stir into chocolate mixture gradually and smoothly. Beat egg whites till they hold a shape, and mix gently into the batter. Pour into pan and bake 15 minutes. Cool thoroughly, then chill. Serve in thin wedges with whipped cream.

There's nothing quite like this. It's not a pudding and not a cake, but a combination of everything good.

CHOCOLATE DESSERT SUPREME #2

1 pound semisweet chocolate
6 eggs, separated
½ pint heavy cream
1 tablespoon liquor (rum, bourbon, sherry,
or crème de cacao)
chopped nuts
whipped cream

Melt chocolate over hot water. Remove from heat. Beat in egg yolks one at a time. Stir cream in slowly. Add liquor very slowly, stirring constantly. Fold in stiffly beaten whites. Pour into shallow serving dish. Sprinkle nuts on top. Chill at least overnight. Serve with flavored whipped cream.

When I first made Chocolate Dessert Supreme #1, I thought that nothing could be as chocolate or as supreme. But then I tried this one. There is a similarity, but this is definitely a pudding and so awfully good it had to be included.

CHOCOLATE MOUSSE #1

½ *pound sweet chocolate*
1 *square unsweetened chocolate*
4 *eggs, separated*
4 *tablespoons sugar*
4 *tablespoons milk*
1 *pint heavy cream*
1 *teaspoon vanilla*

Melt chocolate in top of double boiler. Beat egg yolks, add sugar gradually, beat. Add yolks and milk to melted chocolate and stir till smooth. Pour into bowl and cool. Beat egg whites till stiff but still shiny, and fold into chocolate mixture. Whip cream and fold into mixture with vanilla. Pour into soufflé dish. Chill thoroughly. Sprinkle top with sifted cocoa.

Somebody once told me I should call this "Chocolate Heaven". . . and so it is!

CHOCOLATE MOUSSE #2

1 *pound sweet cooking chocolate, cut up*
2 *ounces unsweetened chocolate, cut up*
7 *tablespoons strong coffee*
2 *tablespoons rum*
5 *eggs, separated*
2 *ounces butter*
1 *cup heavy cream, whipped*
16 *ladyfingers, split*
whipped cream

Put all chocolate and coffee in a heavy pan over a low flame. Stir until the chocolate is dissolved, then add rum. Remove from fire. Add the egg yolks one at a time, then the butter bit by bit. Fold in stiffly beaten egg whites, then whipped cream. Lightly butter the soufflé dish and line bottom and sides with ladyfingers. Fill with mousse and chill overnight. Serve with whipped cream.

Couldn't possibly choose between the first chocolate mousse and this one, so I had to include both. Try each and see what I mean!

CHOCOLATE MOUSSE CRUNCH

CRUST

2 cups chocolate wafers, crushed
⅓ cup melted butter

Mix and press into bottom and sides of 8″ square pan. Bake at 375 for eight minutes. Chill.

MOUSSE

1 cup milk
2 squares unsweetened chocolate
pinch of salt
½ pound (about 32) marshmallows
1 egg yolk, slightly beaten
1 teaspoon vanilla
1 cup heavy cream, whipped

Heat milk, chocolate, salt, and marshmallows over low heat, stirring constantly till chocolate and marshmallows melt. Stir small amount into egg yolk, mixing constantly, then return to hot mixture. Cook and stir over low heat one minute. Add vanilla. Chill till partially set, stirring occasionally. Fold in whipped cream. Pour into crust. Freeze till firm.

Crunchy crust and silky filling—and all chocolate!

POTS DE CRÈME AU CHOCOLAT

2 *cups heavy cream*
2 *cups milk*
1 *cup sugar*
5 *eggs*
5 *egg yolks*
4 *ounces sweet chocolate, melted*
5 *ounces unsweetened chocolate, melted*
1 *tablespoon vanilla*

Heat cream, milk, and half of sugar till skin starts to form. Beat eggs and yolks lightly with remaining sugar. Stir cream into eggs. Add chocolate, then vanilla. Let mixture stand for 15 minutes. Skim foam off top carefully. Spoon into 12 pots. Put pots into deep pan and fill the pan halfway up with boiling water. Cover loosely with another pan. Cook at 350 for 45 minutes. Remove the cover and cook for 15 minutes more. Cool, then chill overnight. Serve with plain or whipped cream.

These are rich and delicious and they look tempting in the little pots. You can freeze any that are left over.

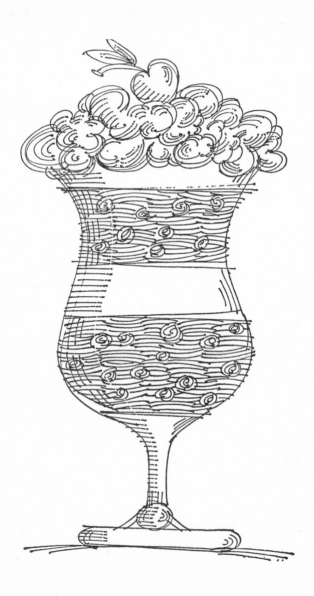

Dreamy Puddings

BAKED CUSTARD

⅔ *cup sweetened condensed milk*
2 *cups hot water*
3 *eggs, slightly beaten*
pinch of salt
1½ *teaspoons vanilla*
nutmeg

Combine milk and water. Stir gradually into eggs. Stir in salt and vanilla. Pour into custard cups. Sprinkle with nutmeg. Place in shallow pan of hot water. Bake at 325 for 1 hour, or till done.

Very simple to make, but creamier and richer than most custards. Vary it by mixing 1 tablespoon instant coffee into the hot water, or by using other flavorings in place of the vanilla.

CHOCOLATE CUSTARD PUDDING

4 eggs
½ cup sugar
1 teaspoon vanilla
1 large can evaporated milk (1⅔ cups)
3 squares unsweetened chocolate
pinch of salt

Set oven at 325. Beat eggs with salt. Stir in half the sugar and the vanilla. Pour the milk into large measuring cup and fill with water till the amount reaches 2¼ cups. Cook the milk, chocolate and rest of sugar together until completely dissolved and well blended (use egg beater to completely dissolve). Add this mixture to eggs. Mix thoroughly. Pour into baking dish and place it in a pan of hot water. Bake for about an hour or till knife inserted in center comes out clean. Chill. Sprinkle sifted cocoa on top.

Much richer than custard, almost like a mousse. This, like all of the puddings, should be cooked and served in a large white soufflé dish.

COFFEE CUSTARD SUPREME

2 quarts milk
1 cup powdered instant coffee
1 tablespoon grated orange rind
5 eggs
5 egg yolks
¾ cup sugar
½ teaspoon salt
1 teaspoon vanilla
1 teaspoon almond flavoring
chopped Brazil nuts

Set oven at 325. Scald milk, add coffee and orange rind. Cool 10 minutes. Beat eggs and egg yolks, sugar, and salt with fork. Add milk, flavorings. Pour into soufflé dish and set in pan of hot water. Bake 1 hour or till set. Chill thoroughly. Sprinkle with nuts. Serves 12.

Lovely ending for a rich dinner. It's impressive, but not too sweet.

EGGNOG PUDDING

1 package vanilla pudding mix
⅛ teaspoon nutmeg
2¼ cups milk
1 egg, separated
1 tablespoon brandy
2 tablespoons sugar

Combine pudding, nutmeg and a quarter-cup of milk in saucepan. Add egg yolk and blend well. Add rest of milk. Cook over medium heat, stirring constantly, till mixture comes to a boil. Remove from heat. Add brandy. Cool for about 5 minutes, stirring now and then. Beat egg white till frothy. Add sugar a little at a time, beating constantly. Fold into eggnog mixture. Pour into custard cups. Sprinkle with nutmeg. Chill.

This makes a nice holiday–time pudding and couldn't be simpler. I find the pudding mixes very acceptable if they're treated right. I always make them with 2¼ cups of milk. Try adding 1 teaspoon instant coffee or a couple of broken-up milk chocolate candy bars to vanilla pudding. . . . Delicious!

RICE PUDDING

4 tablespoons raw rice
7 tablespoons sugar
pinch of salt
1 quart milk
1 teaspoon vanilla
cinnamon

Set oven at 300. Put rice, sugar, salt, and 3 cups of milk into baking dish. Bake for 3 hours or until the consistency is creamy. During first hour stir gently three or four times with fork. During second hour stir gently twice with fork and add the remaining cup of milk. During third hour add vanilla and dash of cinnamon, and stir gently into pudding.

It might appear too soft when first removed from the oven, but it must be cooled and then chilled thoroughly before serving.

Nobody ever believes this pudding isn't made with cream. It tastes very rich, but really isn't.

TAPIOCA PUDDING

1 cup pearl tapioca
4 cups scalded milk
3 eggs, separated
½ cup sugar
½ teaspoon salt
3 teaspoons vanilla

Soak tapioca in cold water to cover for 24 hours. Drain. Cook tapioca in milk in double boiler until clear (about an hour). Add half the sugar to milk and remainder to egg yolks, slightly beaten with salt. Pour hot mixture slowly on egg mixture, stirring. Return to double boiler and stir and cook till thickened. Cool and add vanilla. Fold in stiffly beaten egg whites. Chill.

There's all the difference in the world between the quick cooking tapioca and this. Half the delight is in the texture.

TOAST PUDDING

5 *slices white bread*
6 *eggs*
1 *quart milk*
1 *cup sugar*
2 *teaspoons vanilla*

Set oven at 350. Toast bread; butter; cut in cubes; and place in buttered baking dish. Beat eggs with fork. Add sugar and vanilla and blend well. Add milk and stir till thoroughly mixed. Pour over toast cubes and set baking dish in pan of hot water. Bake for about an hour and 15 minutes, or till set.

I suppose you could call it plain bread pudding, but it's a little more special.

TRIFLE PUDDING

1¾ cups milk
3 tablespoons flour
2 egg yolks
¼ cup sugar
½ teaspoon salt
1 teaspoon vanilla
2 dozen ladyfingers
blueberry jam
6 tablespoons sherry
6 almond macaroons, crumbled
1 cup heavy cream
1 tablespoon sugar
toasted slivered almonds

Heat 1¼ cups of milk till skin forms on top. Mix remaining ½ cup milk into flour till smooth, then stir into hot milk. Cook almost to boiling point. Beat egg yolks slightly. Add sugar and salt gradually, and beat again with beater till mixture is smooth. Stir hot milk mixture into egg yolk mixture very slowly, stirring constantly. Cook over gently boiling water, stirring frequently, till custard is smooth and thick enough to coat a spoon. Add vanilla and chill. Split ladyfingers, spread with jam, and put together again. Arrange half the ladyfingers in rows on the bottom and standing upright against the sides of a serving dish. Sprinkle with 3 tablespoons of the sherry. Place the remaining ladyfingers in rows running in the opposite direction, and sprinkle with rest of sherry. Pour chilled custard over all, then crumble the macaroons on top. Whip the cream with the tablespoon of sugar, spread over top and stick the almonds upright all over the surface.

Absolutely delicious!

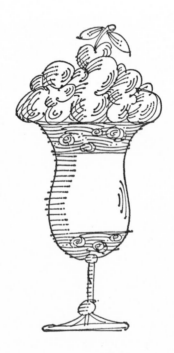

Fruit Delights

DRIED FRUIT COMPOTE

¾ pound mixed dried fruits
1 cup raisins
3 cups water
⅓ cup sugar
juice of 1 lemon
1 orange
sour cream

Wash and drain fruits. Combine in casserole with water. Bake at 325 for 1 hour. Add sugar and lemon juice and stir till sugar is dissolved. Peel and thinly slice the orange, then add. Cool, chill thoroughly, and serve with sour cream.

Long chilling is necessary for the juice to become syrupy, so be patient. Wonderful served right along with meats for a buffet dinner.

FRUIT MELANGE

apples, pears, bananas, cut in pieces
berries
raisins
nuts
honey
lemon juice
sour cream

Combine fruits and nuts. Add honey and lemon juice to taste. Stir in sour cream.

I haven't given exact measurements because this is a good ad lib dessert. Make it for one or for fifty. Go by taste. With this combination, you can't go wrong.

FRUIT MOUSSE

*1 package frozen strawberries,
    raspberries, or peaches*
1 cup sugar
1 teaspoon vanilla
1 pint sour cream

Thaw berries or peaches. Combine them in electric blender with all other ingredients. When thoroughly blended pour into ice tray and freeze till solid but not hard.

Nicer than ice cream. The trick is to serve it soft and creamy, never too hard.

FRUIT WITH MACAROON TOPPING

>*1 package frozen whole strawberries*
>*1 package frozen sliced peaches*
>*1 package frozen raspberries*
>*1 package frozen chunk pineapple*
>*2 bananas*
>*1 pint sour cream*
>*¼ cup brown sugar*
>*1 dozen almond macaroons, crumbled*

Thaw fruits and add sliced bananas. Combine sour cream, sugar, and macaroons and chill several hours. Serve topping in separate bowl.

Great combination, great taste! Good do-it-ahead party dessert for twelve.

FRUIT WITH SOFT CUSTARD

> *fresh sliced peaches*
> *strawberries*
> *blueberries*
> *boysenberries*
> *1 cup milk*
> *1 cup heavy cream*
> *4 egg yolks*
> *¼ cup sugar*
> *1 tablespoon flour*
> *pinch of salt*
> *1½ teaspoons vanilla*

Combine any of these fruits, or all. Fresh are preferred, with possibly one package of frozen. Heat milk with cream in top of double boiler till tiny bubbles appear. Beat yolks slightly with fork, stir in sugar, flour, and salt. Add hot milk mixture very slowly, stirring constantly. Return to double boiler and cook over hot water, stirring, till custard coats the spoon. Cool, add vanilla, chill. Serve in pitcher to pour over fruit.

Soft custard is one of those lovely things I could pour over anything. However, it's best over this combination of fruits.

FRUIT WITH SOUR CREAM

seedless grapes
sliced peaches
strawberries
sour cream
brown sugar

Use any one, two, or all of the fruits. Layer in soufflé dish with sour cream. Sprinkle each layer with brown sugar. Chill for at least two hours.

After it has set a while, the brown sugar melts into the cream and becomes something heavenly!

ITALIAN CREAM CHEESE WITH FRUIT

fresh fruits, cut in pieces
1 cup cottage cheese
½ cup sour cream
1 tablespoon sugar
1 tablespoon rum
cinnamon

Combine fruits in serving dish. Blend all ingredients except cinnamon, and mound in bowl. Just before serving, sprinkle top of mound with cinnamon and serve as topping for fruit.

Try apples and pears but nothing too soft. Makes a fine dessert after a spaghetti dinner.

SWEDISH CREAM WITH BERRIES

1 *envelope gelatin*
1 *pint heavy cream*
1 *cup sugar*
1 *pint sour cream*
1 *teaspoon vanilla*
2 *packages frozen raspberries, thawed*
1 *package frozen whole boysenberries, thawed*

Sprinkle gelatin on a quarter-cup of the cream till completely softened. Mix with rest of cream and sugar over low heat and stir till gelatin is completely dissolved. Cool till slightly thickened. Fold in sour cream and vanilla. Pour into soufflé dish and chill till set. Cover with berries.

Beautiful smooth cream . . . a sensational base for berries.

Good and Hot

APRICOT PANCAKES

PANCAKES

3 eggs
1 teaspoon salt
1½ teaspoons sugar
1 cup sifted all-purpose flour
2 cups milk
3 tablespoons melted butter

Beat eggs till light. Add salt and sugar, beating constantly. Add flour, milk, and butter. Beat till smooth. Pour into pitcher. Heat small skillet till very hot. Rub with small amount of butter on piece of wax paper. Pour in very small amount of batter. Tilt pan quickly so entire bottom is covered thinly, and cook over medium heat till underside is delicately browned. Turn over with spatula. Brown other side, then transfer to paper towels to cool. When cool, place between rounds of freezer paper. Stack, wrap in freezer foil, and freeze till ready to use. Makes about 21 pancakes.

SAUCE

2 cans apricot nectar
grated rind of 1 orange
juice of 1 lemon
2 tablespoons butter

Place all ingredients in saucepan and cook uncovered for 5 minutes.

Thaw pancakes at room temperature. Spread thinly with apricot jam. Roll and place in oblong baking dish side by side (do not stack). Spoon some of sauce over pancakes. Place them in 350 oven till hot. Keep rest of sauce hot to pour over each serving.

Such an elegant dessert, and made very simple by the freezing procedure.

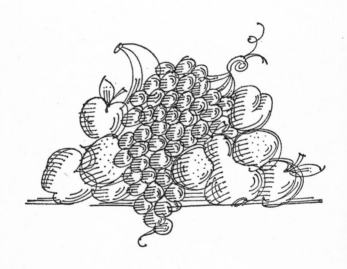

BAKED PEACH DESSERT

6 *large ripe peaches, sliced*
3 *tablespoons butter*
1 *cup sugar*
2 *eggs*
1 *cup sifted flour*
pinch of salt
1 *tablespoon baking powder*
1 *teaspoon vanilla*
1 *cup heavy cream, whipped*
¼ *teaspoon almond flavoring*

Set oven at 350. Place peach slices in bottom of greased soufflé dish. Cream the butter, add the sugar, then eggs. Do not beat, just mix till blended. Sift flour with salt and baking powder and add. Add vanilla. Pour batter over peaches and bake for one hour. Serve with almond flavored whipped cream.

Also good with plain heavy cream, not whipped. The fruit is tart, the cake is sweet, and the texture is marvelous!

BANANA CAKE

¼ pound butter, softened
1¼ cups sugar
2 eggs, beaten
1 teaspoon soda
4 tablespoons sour cream
1½ cups sifted cake flour
¼ teaspoon salt
1 cup banana puree
1 teaspoon vanilla

Set oven at 350. Grease a 11 x 8 x 2 oblong baking pan and flour lightly. Cream butter and sugar well. Add eggs, then soda dissolved in sour cream. Beat well. Stir in alternately the flour mixed with the salt and the banana purée. Add vanilla and mix. Bake for about 30 minutes or till done. Serve warm with sweetened whipped cream and sliced bananas, or softened banana ice cream.

This cake is also good served cold with chocolate or white frosting.

CARAMEL CREAM PEARS

6 *very firm pears*
¾ *cup sugar*
2 *tablespoons butter*
1 *cup heavy cream*

Set oven at 475. Cut pears into quarters, core and peel. Arrange in a buttered baking dish (not glass). Sprinkle sugar over pears, dot with butter. Bake for 30 minutes or till sugar turns dark brown. Baste frequently after sugar and butter have melted. Pour cream over and stir gently with rubber spatula. Cook for 5 minutes more. Pour into heated soufflé dish and serve hot.

Don't be disturbed if you have a little left over. I had a portion of it cold one day and it was beautiful!

CHOCOLATE SOUFFLÉ

6 tablespoons butter
4 squares unsweetened chocolate
½ cup sifted flour
2 cups milk
1⅓ cups sugar
6 eggs, separated
¼ teaspoon salt
2 teaspoons vanilla

Melt butter with chocolate over low heat. Blend in flour and salt. Add milk and half the sugar. Cook, stirring, for about 20 minutes or till thickened. Blend in beaten egg yolks and vanilla. Refrigerate till needed.

Set oven at 425. Reheat chocolate mixture over boiling water, stirring. Remove from heat. Beat egg whites till they stand in moist, drooping peaks. Add the rest of sugar gradually and beat till stiff. Fold into chocolate mixture. Pour into soufflé dish. Set in shallow pan of hot water. Bake for about 45 minutes, or till done. Serve with softened vanilla ice cream.

If I had to pick my favorite dessert of all, I guess I'd pick this one. The combination of texture, taste, aroma, and sheer beauty can't be beat.

NOODLE NUT PUDDING

1 eight-ounce package thin noodles
4 tablespoons butter
1 cup chopped walnuts
½ cup pineapple juice
½ cup maple syrup
2 tablespoons brown sugar
1 teaspoon cinnamon
½ teaspoon nutmeg
1 teaspoon vanilla
3 tablespoons brown sugar

Set oven at 350. Cook noodles in salted boiling water till just tender. Drain. Melt butter. Add all ingredients except final 3 tablespoons brown sugar. Stir mixture into noodles. Put in a shallow baking dish. Sprinkle with remaining brown sugar. Bake for 40 minutes. Place under broiler for a few minutes, watching carefully. Serve hot with a dollop of sour cream on each serving.

Serves 6.

Especially good after a light dinner. It's substantial and very tasty.

PEACH KUCHEN

2 cups sifted all-purpose flour
¼ teaspoon salt
½ cup sugar
¼ pound butter, softened
1 teaspoon baking powder
12 canned peach halves
1 teaspoon cinnamon
2 egg yolks
1 cup sour cream

Set oven at 400. Sift together flour, baking powder, salt, and 3 tablespoons of the sugar. Cut in butter till mealy. Spread an even layer of this mixture over bottom and halfway up the sides of an 8-inch square pan, using your hands. Press dough firmly until it holds. Drain peaches thoroughly, then arrange over bottom pastry neatly and sprinkle with mixture of remaining sugar and cinnamon. Bake 15 minutes. Then pour a mixture of slightly beaten egg yolks and sour cream over the top. Bake 30 minutes longer. Serve hot with a dollop of sour cream on each serving.

I always think of this as a winter dessert, but of course it's good at any time. Rather than try to time its emergence from the oven with the completion of the main course, I suggest baking it in advance, freezing it in serving-size pieces, and then heating in a low oven.

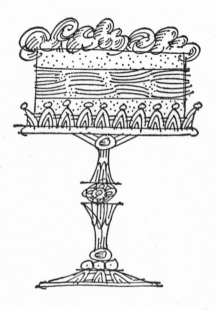

PUMPKIN PUDDING

¾ cup sugar
1 tablespoon flour
½ teaspoon salt
1½ teaspoons cinnamon
½ teaspoon nutmeg
½ teaspoon ground cloves
1½ cups pumpkin
2 eggs
1 can evaporated milk (1⅔ ounces)

Set oven at 350. Combine sugar, flour, salt, and spices. Ad pumpkin. Mix well. Beat eggs lightly, add milk. Add to pumpkin mixture and blend well. Pour into greased baking dish and set in pan of hot water. Bake for about 45 minutes or till knife inserted in center comes out clean. Serve hot with softened vanilla ice cream as topping.

A nice holiday dessert, and a good change from pumpkin pie. Can also be served with whipped cream sprinkled with nutmeg.

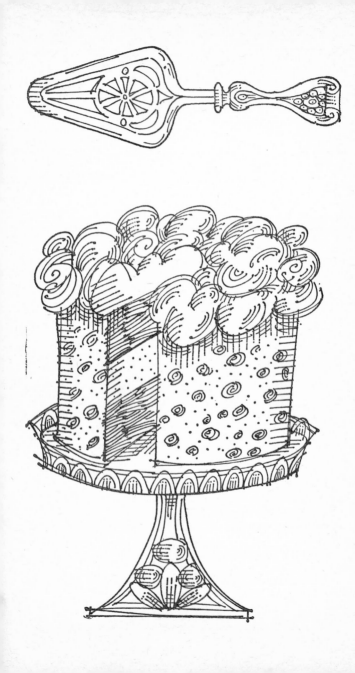

Lovely Cakes

CINNAMON CAKE

CAKE

¼ pound butter, softened
1 cup sugar
2 eggs
1½ cups sifted all-purpose flour
¼ teaspoon salt
1½ teaspoons baking powder
1 cup sour cream
1 teaspoon baking soda

TOPPING

½ cup brown sugar
1½ tablespoons cinnamon
½ cup slivered almonds

Set oven at 350. Grease 8-inch square pan. Cream butter well with sugar. Add eggs, mix. Sift flour together with salt and baking powder, and add to mixture alternately with sour cream to which baking soda has been added. Spread half of batter in pan. Sprinkle with half of topping. Spread on rest of batter. Sprinkle with rest of topping. Bake for 45 minutes or till done.

Somehow I can't be bothered with complicated coffee cakes that have to rise or be rolled out. This is

a simple cake to make and serves the purpose per-
fectly. It will stay fresh for a long time—but I believe
in tossing everything into the freezer oven-fresh, and
then thawing it when it's needed.

GOLD CAKE

½ pound butter, softened
2 cups sugar
6 egg yolks
yellow food coloring
1 tablespoon vanilla
3½ cups sifted flour
1½ teaspoons baking powder
pinch of salt
1 cup milk
poppy seeds

Set oven at 350. Grease, line with waxed paper, and grease again a 9-inch tube pan. Beat butter and sugar till creamy. Add egg yolks, a few drops of food coloring, and vanilla. Add flour sifted with baking powder and salt alternately with milk. Fold in sprinkling of poppy seeds. Bake an hour and 15 minutes, or till done.

Similar in texture to pound cake. This is an excellent plain cake. Try it with orange or lemon flavoring, too.

JAM CAKE

¾ cup cooking oil
¾ cup sugar
4 eggs
1½ cups sifted cake flour
2 teaspoons baking powder
pinch of salt
1 teaspoon vanilla
jam

Set oven at 375. Grease and lightly flour two 8-inch round cake pans. Beat oil and sugar well. Add eggs one at a time, beating very well after each addition. Sift flour, baking powder, and salt together, then add to batter gradually. Add vanilla and mix well. Bake for 20 minutes, or till done. When thoroughly cool split both layers. Spread jam generously between each layer and stack. Sift powdered sugar over top.

Wonderful with blackberry or strawberry preserves or any good jam.

ORANGE CAKE

¼ pound butter, softened
1 cup sugar
2 eggs
½ pint sour cream
1 whole medium orange, ground
1 teaspoon soda
2½ cups sifted cake flour
1 teaspoon vanilla

Set oven at 350. Grease and lightly flour a 9-inch square pan. Cream together butter and sugar. Beat in eggs, sour cream, orange (with juice), and soda. Add flour and blend well. Add vanilla. Bake for 40 minutes or till done.

Such a good true orange flavor. . . . It's marvelous served just as is; or top it with a lemon glaze (see Carrot Cake) or white frosting.

POUND CAKE

½ pound butter, softened
1¾ cups sugar
5 eggs
2 cups sifted all-purpose flour
½ teaspoon salt
3 teaspoons vanilla
1 teaspoon orange flavoring

Set oven at 325. Grease large loaf pan. Line bottom with wax paper and grease again. Cream butter and sugar well. Add eggs one at a time and beat well. Sift flour with salt, and add to mixture. Add flavorings. Bake for 2 hours or till done.

Here is a cake you can do things with. Of course, it's great just as is, straight from the oven, or cooled. But try it toasted some morning with your coffee. Or spread it with jam. Vary it by tossing a sprinkling of either poppy or caraway seeds into the mixed batter before baking (stir in well, of course), or substitute a teaspoon of almond or lemon flavoring instead of the orange. Slice the cake when it's cooled and wrap two or three pieces together in foil paper and freeze. Then you can take out just the amount needed at a time and either thaw at room temperature or warm in a very low oven.

SPICE CAKE

¾ cup butter, softened
1 cup dark brown sugar
4 eggs
¼ cup sour milk
2 cups sifted cake flour
1 teaspoon soda
1 teaspoon baking powder
1 teaspoon nutmeg
1 teaspoon cinnamon
1 teaspoon ground cloves
1 cup seedless blackberry jam

Set oven at 350. Grease and flour a 13 x 9 x 2 oblong pan. Cream butter and sugar. Add eggs one at a time. Add milk. Sift all dry ingredients together and add. Mix in jam. Bake for 40 minutes or till done. When cool, spread with a layer of jam or glaze (see Carrot Cake).

Very moist and very flavorful!

WHITE CAKE

2¼ cups sifted cake flour
3 teaspoons baking powder
½ teaspoon salt
1½ cups sugar
¼ pound butter, softened
1 cup milk, minus 2 tablespoons
4 egg whites
1 teaspoon vanilla
½ teaspoon almond flavoring

Set oven at 350. Grease and lightly flour a 11 x 8 x 2 oblong pan. Sift together flour, baking powder, salt, and sugar. Add butter and three-quarters of the milk. Beat. Add rest of milk, egg whites, and flavorings. Beat again. Bake for 30 minutes or till done. Cool, then frost with any topping that suits your mood.

Snowy white and lovely to look at, delightful to taste.

YELLOW CAKE

2¼ cups sifted cake flour
3 teaspoons baking powder
½ teaspoon salt
1½ cups sugar
¼ pound butter, softened
1 cup milk, minus 2 tablespoons
2 eggs
1½ teaspoons vanilla

Set oven at 350. Grease and lightly flour a 11 x 8 x 2 oblong pan. Sift together flour, baking powder, salt, and sugar. Add butter and three-quarters of the milk. Beat. Add rest of milk, eggs, and vanilla. Beat again. Bake for about 30 minutes or till done. Cool. Turn out and cover with white frosting and sprinkle with cocoanut.

Vary this cake by using different frostings—chocolate, mocha, or anything good.

Luscious Frostings

BITTERSWEET FROSTING

1 egg white
¾ cup sugar
2½ tablespoons cold water
pinch of salt
pinch of cream of tartar
1 teaspoon white Karo syrup
1 teaspoon vanilla
1½ squares unsweetened chocolate, melted

Place all ingredients but vanilla and chocolate over rapidly boiling water. Beat constantly for about 6 minutes with electric beater until frosting will form peaks. Remove from heat. Add vanilla. Beat until right consistency for spreading on cake. After cake is frosted, drip melted chocolate over top and swirl into frosting with knife.

This is a pretty frosting. And you can vary the effect and taste by how much of the chocolate you blend into the white.

CARAMEL FROSTING

¾ stick butter
¾ cup brown sugar
pinch of salt
3 tablespoons milk
2 cups powdered sugar
1 teaspoon vanilla

Combine butter, brown sugar, and salt in saucepan over low heat. Boil for 2 minutes, stirring constantly. Add milk, return to boil, remove from heat. Cool slightly. Add powdered sugar and beat until thick enough to spread. Add vanilla.

Always good on yellow or white cakes, but try it on Spice or Ginger Cake.

CHOCOLATE FROSTING

1 cup light cream
1 cup sugar
1 cup Ghiradelli's ground chocolate
pinch of salt
⅓ stick butter
1 teaspoon vanilla

Mix all ingredients except butter and vanilla in a heavy pot. Then boil slowly for about 45 minutes, or to the soft-ball stage. Take off fire and add butter and vanilla. Set aside to cool for a few minutes. Beat. Spread on cake.

This is a really marvelous frosting, shiny and black and very fudgy.

COFFEE FROSTING

3 teaspoons instant coffee
¼ cup hot water
4 tablespoons butter
2 cups sifted powdered sugar

Dissolve coffee in hot water. In a large bowl, cream butter. Stir in 3 teaspoons of liquid and 1 cup of the sugar. Gradually add remaining sugar and liquid. Beat till frosting is smooth and creamy.

Not very fancy, but very tasty. Especially nice on a yellow cake cut into small squares.

FRENCH BUTTER FROSTING

3 squares unsweetened chocolate
2 tablespoons butter
⅓ cup milk
1¼ cups sifted powdered sugar
1 teaspoon vanilla
1 egg

Dissolve chocolate in top of double boiler over hot water. Add butter and milk and mix. Remove from water and fill bottom of double boiler with ice cubes and cold water. Add sugar, vanilla, and egg to chocolate mixture and beat it for one minute at room temperature. Then put it over the ice cubes and beat with electric mixer at high speed for about 15 minutes, till frosting is thick and light in color. Spread on completely cooled cake.

It takes time, but with an electric beater it's not too much trouble, and it's certainly worth it.

MOCHA FROSTING

½ pound butter, softened
¼ cup cocoa
2 teaspoons instant coffee
1 egg
1 teaspoon vanilla
pinch of salt
3½ cups sifted powdered sugar

Add cocoa and coffee to butter and blend well. Add egg, vanilla, and salt. Beat till well combined. Add sugar a little at a time, beating well after each addition.

Exceptionally rich and thick, good enough to eat with a spoon!

WHIPPED CREAM AND JAM FROSTING

1 cup heavy cream
1 cup raspberry jam

Whip cream till stiff. Fold in jam. Spread on cake. Keep refrigerated.

This frosting looks as lovely as it tastes. Try it on the White Cake. Good on the Yellow, too.

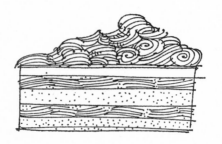

WHITE FROSTING

1 egg white
¾ cup sugar
2½ tablespoons cold water
pinch of salt
pinch of cream of tartar
1 teaspoon white Karo syrup
1 teaspoon vanilla
shredded cocoanut

Place all ingredients except vanilla in top of double boiler over rapidly boiling water. Beat constantly with electric mixer till mixture will form peaks. Remove from heat. Add vanilla. Beat till right consistency for spreading on cake. After spreading on cake, sprinkle with cocoanut.

Try different flavorings besides cocoanut and add a couple of drops of food coloring.

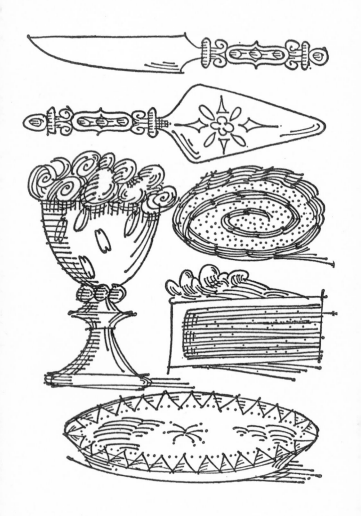

Sheer Delight

BUTTER PECAN MOUSSE

2 tablespoons unflavored gelatin
½ cup cold water
two 14½-ounce cans of evaporated milk
¾ cup sugar
4 ounces pecans, chopped
4 tablespoons butter
1 tablespoon vanilla

Soften gelatin in cold water. Mix milk and sugar, scald. Add softened gelatin, stir until dissolved. Chill thoroughly. Brown pecans in butter, cool. Beat chilled milk mixture with electric beater till almost stiff. Fold in nuts and vanilla. Freeze till firm.

Marvelous flavor! Very pretty if you let it set in a fancy mold.

CHEESE CAKE

18 zwieback, crushed into crumbs
½ cup sugar
¼ pound butter, melted
1 pint cottage cheese
¼ cup sifted flour
4 eggs
¼ teaspoon salt
1 cup sugar
1 cup cream
1 teaspoon vanilla

Set oven at 325. Mix zwieback and sugar together. Add butter and mix. Pack into bottom and sides of an 8-inch square pan. Mix cheese and flour in small bowl with electric mixer. Beat eggs with salt in large bowl, add sugar, and beat till thick and light in color. Add cheese, cream, and vanilla, and beat with mixer till thoroughly blended. Pour into pan and bake for one hour. Turn off oven and leave cake inside for one more hour; don't open oven door. Cool, and chill.

As in the making of Martinis, everyone feels that his way of making cheese cake is the right way. I think it's strictly a matter of taste—and this is the taste that I like.

CHOCOLATE CREAM CHEESE PIE

2 *cups vanilla cookie crumbs, finely crushed*
⅓ *cup butter, melted*
1 *cup heavy cream*
3 *tablespoons cocoa*
2 *teaspoons sugar*
12 *ounces semisweet chocolate*
2 *eight-ounce packages of cream cheese, softened*
½ *cup strong coffee*
pinch of salt
1 *teaspoon vanilla*
4 *eggs, separated*
⅔ *cup sugar*
chopped nuts (optional)

Stir butter into cookie crumbs and press into bottom and sides of well-greased spring-form pan. Chill. Mix cocoa and 2 teaspoons sugar into cream (don't whip), and chill. Set oven at 350. Melt chocolate in double boiler over hot water. Ad coffee gradually to cream cheese, and beat till smooth. Add salt and vanilla. Mix into melted chocolate and stir till smooth. Remove from heat and cool for five minutes, stirring occasionally. Beat yolks with half of sugar till thick and lemon colored. Slowly add chocolate mixture to yolks. Beat whites with remaining sugar till stiff but not dry. Fold into the batter and pour into chilled shell. Bake for 1 hour or till set. Turn off heat, open oven door, and let cake cool in oven. Chill. Remove sides of pan. Whip cream till stiff and spread over top. Sprinkle with chopped nuts.

Terribly, terribly rich . . . make the servings small.

CHOCOLATE ROLL

CAKE

4 *eggs, separated*
5 *tablespoons sugar*
3 *tablespoons sifted flour*
granulated sugar

Set oven at 350. Grease a baking sheet well. Line with wax paper, grease again. In small bowl beat egg yolks slightly. Add flour and sugar and beat well. Gently fold this mixture into stiffly beaten egg whites. Spread mixture evenly in pan. Bake 17 minutes. Sprinkle generously with granulated sugar. Loosen cake with spatula. Invert onto wax paper. Remove paper. Roll up cake. Refrigerate.

FILLING

6 *squares semisweet chocolate*
½ *square unsweetened chocolate*
3 *tablespoons cold water*
3 *tablespoons soft butter*
1 *teaspoon vanilla*
1 *teaspoon rum*
½ *square semisweet chocolate, grated coarsely*
powdered sugar

Over low heat melt semisweet and unsweetened chocolate, stirring with cold water till dissolved and smooth. Remove from heat and stir in soft butter, vanilla, and rum. Set in bowl of ice. Stir till mixture is cold and slightly thickened. Unroll cake. Spread with three-quarters of mixture, roll up. Frost with rest. Sprinkle with grated chocolate, then powdered sugar.

Make the serving small on this one. It's extremely rich, almost candylike.

COFFEE CREAM ROLL

FILLING

1 cup heavy cream
3 tablespoons sugar
1½ tablespoons instant coffee
½ teaspoon vanilla

Mix (don't whip) ingredients for filling. Chill in refrigerator for 1 or 2 hours.

CAKE

3 eggs, separated
5 tablespoons sugar
2 tablespoons instant coffee
1 teaspoon vanilla

Set oven at 350. Grease an 8-inch square pan and line with wax paper; grease again. Beat egg yolks thoroughly with beater. Add sugar gradually and continue beating till mixture is very creamy. Add instant coffee and vanilla, and mix. Beat egg whites till they hold a peak. Mix batter in gently. Pour into pan and bake for about 30 minutes or till cake pulls away from sides of pan. Cool 5 minutes. Remove from pan, peel off paper, and let cake cool on rack. Whip cream filling mixture till it holds a shape. Spread half on cake. Bring two sides up together to form a roll. Frost with remaining cream. Sprinkle with chocolate sprinkles or chopped pistachio nuts. Serve immediately.

For simpler serving: When roll is completed, set on sheet of foil paper and put in freezer (unwrapped) till cream hardens slightly. Then wrap securely. When you want to serve it, cut the roll in slices while it's still frozen, and let thaw in refrigerator or at room temperature till cream is almost, not quite, soft again. Very unusual and delicious!

CRÈME BRÛLÉE

2 cups light cream
5 egg yolks
3 tablespoons sugar
1 teaspoon vanilla
brown sugar, sifted

Scald cream in top of double boiler over low flame. Beat yolks till light. Add sugar and vanilla and beat till creamy. Stir warm cream into egg mixture very slowly. Pour back into double boiler. Place over boiling water and stir till custard thickens and coats spoon. Pour into soufflé dish and refrigerate till set and thoroughly chilled. Sprinkle top thickly with brown sugar. Place dish in bowl of ice and place both under broiler till sugar hardens. The flame should not be too high, and watch very closely for burning. Rechill.

This is wonderfully good just as is, but it also makes a nice summer dessert spooned over fresh berries.

LIME PIE

CRUST

1⅓ cups graham cracker crumbs
¼ cup sugar
⅓ cup melted butter

Mix these three ingredients together. Press into pie
dish. Bake at 375 for 8 minutes. Chill.

FILLING

½ cup lime juice
1 teaspoon lime rind
1 fifteen-ounce can condensed milk
2 egg yolks

Combine juice with rind and stir into condensed
milk. Add yolks, blend. Pour into crust and chill.

TOPPING

1 cup heavy cream
2 tablespoons sugar
½ teaspoon vanilla

Beat ingredients till thickened, not stiff. Pour over
filling.

*This is the kind of pie I like—quick and simple to
make. Freezes beautifully.*

MAPLE MOUSSE

5 egg yolks
1½ cups maple syrup, hot
1 teaspoon vanilla
1 pint heavy cream, whipped

Beat yolks till light and lemon-colored. Put in top of double boiler over boiling water and add hot maple syrup gradually, beating constantly with spoon. Cook and beat till custard coats spoon. Remove from flame. Set top of double boiler in bowl of ice and continue beating till mousse is cool and thick. Add vanilla. Fold in whipped cream. Pour into soufflé dish and freeze.

Sweet and rich and creamy. Don't let it get too hard; if it does, thaw it a bit before serving.

Some Marvelous Things

BUTTERSCOTCH PUDDING

1 package butterscotch pudding
1 tablespoon instant coffee
2¼ cups cream

Mix ingredients together and cook according to package instructions.

Can you believe anything that simple can be that good? The cream makes the difference.

CHOCOLATE ICE CREAM ROLL

¼ cup sifted cake flour
½ teaspoon salt
5 tablespoons cocoa
1 cup powdered sugar
5 eggs, separated
1 teaspoon vanilla

Set oven at 400. Line greased sheet pan with wax paper. Sift flour, salt, cocoa, and sugar together three times. Beat egg yolks till thick, and fold the dry ingredients into them. Beat egg whites till stiff, add vanilla, and fold them into batter. Spread in pan. Bake 15 to 20 minutes and turn out on damp cloth. Remove paper, cut off hard edges, and roll up cake. When cake is cooled, unroll, spread with softened vanilla ice cream, and roll up again. Slice and serve with hot chocolate sauce.

Try pistachio ice cream sometime, or banana nut, peppermint, or coffee—you can't go wrong. For simpler serving, freeze in advance. And if by any chance there's any left over after serving, pile it into a refrigerator tray and keep it semifrozen; it makes a lovely pudding.

FRENCH ICEBOX CAKE

2 *squares unsweetened chocolate*
1 *can sweetened condensed milk*
6 *marshmallows*
½ *cup water*
1 *package chocolate wafers*

Melt chocolate in double boiler. Add milk and stir for 5 minutes until thickened. Add water and marshmallows and let marshmallows melt. Line small loaf pan with waxed paper. Pour layer of chocolate mixture on bottom. Add layer of wafers. Repeat till all mixture is used. Top with layer of wafers. Refrigerate for 24 hours. Turn out on platter and carefully remove paper. Top with flavored whipped cream and sprinkling of sifted cocoa.

Smooth and rich and terribly good.

JAM SQUARES

CAKE

1 cup sifted all purpose flour
1 teaspoon baking powder
3 tablespoons sugar
¼ pound butter
1 egg
1 tablespoon milk
1 tablespoon vanilla
½ cup raspberry jam

Set oven at 350. Grease an 8-inch square pan. Sift flour, baking powder, and sugar together into bowl. Cut in butter till mealy. Beat egg slightly with milk and vanilla, add to flour mixture, and mix well. Spread dough over bottom of pan. Cover with layer of jam.

TOPPING

4 tablespoons butter
1 egg
½ cup sugar, minus 3 tablespoons
1 can shredded cocoanut
1 teaspoon vanilla

Melt butter. Beat egg till frothy, then beat in sugar, then butter. Mix thoroughly. Cut cocoanut into small pieces and add to egg mixture with vanilla. Spread on top of jam. Bake 30 minutes. Let cool thoroughly before cutting into squares.

This is the closest I get to making cookies. These are quite rich and full of personality.

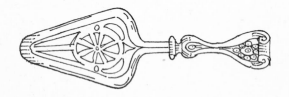

JELLY ROLL

4 eggs
¼ teaspoon salt
1 teaspoon baking powder
¾ cup sugar
¾ cup sifted cake flour
1 teaspoon vanilla

Set oven at 400. Line greased baking sheet with wax paper, then grease again. Mix eggs, salt, and baking powder with electric beater till eggs are foamy. Continue beating at high speed, adding sugar very slowly. Beat till very thick and tripled in volume. Fold in flour and vanilla. Pour into pan, leaving slight depression in center. Bake 13 minutes or until light brown. Dust towel with powdered sugar. When cake is done, loosen it from sides of pan and invert it on towel. Peel off paper, cut crisp edges off. Roll up cake, rolling towel up in it. Cool 10 minutes. Unroll. Spread with jelly or jam to within a half-inch of edges. Roll. Wrap towel tightly around roll to shape it. Let cool thoroughly on wire rack before cutting.

There is no end to the variations of flavor here, depending on the kind of filling used, but my preference is a very good blueberry preserve.

STRAWBERRY SHORTCAKE

2 cups sifted flour
¼ cup sugar
4 teaspoons baking powder
½ teaspoon salt
sprinkling of nutmeg
¼ pound butter
1 egg, beaten
⅓ cup milk
3 boxes fresh strawberries and 1 cup sugar, or,
4 packages frozen strawberries
1 cup heavy cream, whipped

Set oven at 450. Grease an 8-inch round cake pan. Sift dry ingredients. Work butter into flour mixture with two knives till consistency of corn meal. Mix in beaten egg, then gradually add milk. Dump dough into baking pan and pat down with your palm to fit the pan. Bake 12 minutes. Cool thoroughly on cake rack. If fresh strawberries are used (and they are certainly preferable), reserve a few whole ones and crush the rest slightly, sprinkle with sugar and refrigerate till needed. Split cooled cake and spread fruit generously between the layers and on top. Cover with whipped cream and garnish with whole berries.

Try this sometime with softened strawberry ice cream in place of the whipped cream.

STRAWBERRY-LEMON TART

TART SHELL

¼ cup butter, softened
1 tablespoon sugar
3 tablespoons almond paste
½ teaspoon grated lemon peel
1 egg white
¾ cup sifted flour

Grease and lightly flour an 8-inch round cake pan. In small bowl mix with electric mixer at medium speed the butter, sugar, almond paste, and lemon peel. Add egg white and beat at high speed till smooth. Add flour gradually, beating till smooth. Turn dough into pan. With back of spoon, pat dough evenly out on the bottom and up the side of the pan. Refrigerate one hour. Meanwhile, make the filling:

FILLING

¼ cup butter
2 eggs, beaten
rind and juice of one large lemon
½ cup sugar

Melt butter in top of double boiler over hot water. Add eggs, rind and juice, and sugar. Cook and stir till smooth and thick. Cool, then chill thoroughly.

Bake the chilled tart shell at 300 for 50 minutes or

till a light golden brown. Cool 15 minutes. Turn out on rack, cool completely.

Wash, hull, and thoroughly drain 1½ boxes of fresh strawberries.

APRICOT GLAZE

Heat and stir 5 tablespoons apricot jam over low flame till smooth. Do not let it come to boil. Strain and cool slightly.

Pour filling into tart shell. Place strawberries all over top, cut some into pieces to fill up small spaces. Cover with glaze. Chill.

This is no one-two-three dessert; but it's well worth the time, and it can be made in advance and frozen.

WALNUT TORTE

CAKE

¼ *pound butter, softened*
¾ *cup sugar*
2 *eggs*
¾ *cup sifted cake flour*
½ *teaspoon vanilla*

Set oven at 375. Grease an 8-inch square pan. Beat butter and sugar together till creamy and light. Add eggs one at a time, and beat some more. Fold in flour. Add vanilla. Pour batter into pan and bake for 25 minutes.

TOPPING

¼ *cup butter*
3 *tablespoons sugar*
2 *tablespoons light cream*
¾ *cup chopped walnuts*
1 *tablespoon flour*

In saucepan over medium heat combine butter, sugar, cream, and half of walnuts. Stir till warm and creamy. Add flour. Simmer for half a minute, remove from heat. When cake has baked 25 minutes, remove it from oven, spread nut mixture over top, and sprinkle with rest of nuts. Bake 20 minutes more. Cool before removing from pan.

This not only freezes beautifully, but it's delicious partially thawed and chewy.

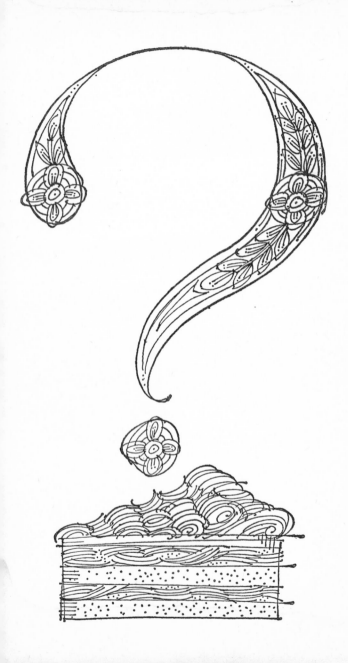

"What's in This Cake?"

CARROT CAKE

CAKE

3 medium carrots, grated
1⅔ cups finely-ground blanched almonds
¾ cup bread crumbs
¼ teaspoon ground cloves
6 eggs, separated
1¼ cups sugar
juice and rind of 1 lemon

Set oven at 350. Grease an 8-inch spring-form pan.
Coat bottom and sides with additional bread crumbs.
Mix carrots, nuts, bread crumbs, cinnamon, and cloves
together in a large bowl. Beat egg yolks, sugar, lemon
juice, and rind with electric beater till thick and
creamy. Beat egg whites till they hold a peak. Stir yolk
mixture into carrot mixture, then fold in whites. Bake
1 hour, or till done.

GLAZE

1 cup powdered sugar
1 tablespoon water
¼ teaspoon lemon flavoring

Mix and spread on completely cooled cake. (Add more water if necessary.)

A cake without butter or flour is quite unusual. This one has a lovely rich texture, and tastes so good.

FARINA CAKE

TOPPING

1½ cups sugar
¾ cup water
1 tablespoon lemon juice

Mix sugar and water together. Bring to full boil, then simmer for about 10 minutes or till syrupy. Remove from heat. Add lemon juice. Chill.

CAKE

¼ pound butter
1 cup sugar
1 cup cream
3 eggs, well beaten
1 teaspoon vanilla
1 cup farina
1 cup sifted all-purpose flour
2 teaspoons baking powder
⅔ cup finely chopped walnuts
½ cup raisins

Set oven at 350. Melt butter in an 8-inch square pan, then pour into mixing bowl. Add sugar and beat thoroughly. Blend in cream, eggs, and vanilla. Combine farina, flour, and baking powder, stir into batter.

Mix in nuts and raisins. Pour into pan and bake for 45 minutes or till done. Cut into squares immediately and pour syrup over all. Let stand several hours before serving.

This is a very unusual cake in flavor and texture.

FIG CAKE

1 pound dried figs
2 tablespoons lemon juice
½ cup sour milk
¼ pound butter, softened
1 cup sugar
2 eggs
2 cups sifted cake flour
1 teaspoon baking powder
1 teaspoon salt
½ teaspoon baking soda
½ teaspoon cinnamon
¼ teaspoon ground cloves
1 teaspoon vanilla

Set oven at 350. Grease and flour a 13 x 9 x 2 oblong baking pan. Wash figs. Add lemon juice and cold water to cover. Boil gently, covered, till figs are soft, about 30 minutes. Cool and drain, reserving the juice. Cut figs into small pieces. Add ½ cup fig juice to milk. Cream butter and sugar. Add eggs, one at a time. Sift all dry ingredients together and add alternately with milk and fig juice. Add figs and vanilla. Bake for 50 minutes or till done.

A tasty rich cake, the only kind of fruit cake I like to make. You can frost it with a plain white icing, but it's just as good without. Freezes well.

GINGER CAKE

CAKE

1 cup dark molasses
¼ pound butter
½ cup brown sugar
½ cup milk
½ cup strong coffee
3 cups sifted cake flour
2 tablespoons ginger
1 tablespoon orange rind
1 teaspoon cinnamon
1 teaspoon mace
1 teaspoon nutmeg
1 teaspoon cream of tartar
1 teaspoon baking soda
3 eggs, very well beaten
½ cup orange juice

Set oven at 350. Grease and line a 13 x 9 x 2 baking pan with wax paper, and grease again. Heat together molasses, butter, brown sugar, milk, and coffee till butter is melted. Sift dry ingredients together into large bowl. Pour molasses mixture in all at once and mix well. Add beaten eggs and orange juice. Pour into pan. Bake for 40 minutes or till done.

TOPPING

1 eight-ounce package cream cheese
2 teaspoons brown sugar
milk or cream
strawberry jam

Mix cream cheese with brown sugar and add enough milk or cream to make it spreadable. Spread on cake, then spread a layer of jam on top.

A great deal better than ordinary gingerbread, and absolutely wonderful when warm.

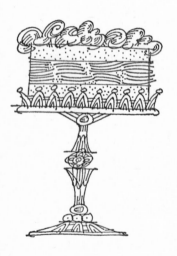

MARMALADE CAKE

¾ cup butter, softened
1 cup sugar
1 tablespoon grated orange rind
2 teaspoons vanilla
3 eggs
1 cup orange marmalade
½ cup white raisins
3 cups sifted all-purpose flour
1½ teaspoons soda
1 teaspoon salt
1 cup buttermilk or sour milk

Set oven at 350. Grease a 9-inch tube pan and line with wax paper, then grease again. Cream together the butter, sugar, orange rind, and vanilla. When light and fluffy, beat in the eggs one at a time. Stir in marmalade and raisins. Sift together flour, soda, and salt. Add to creamed mixture alternately with milk. Turn batter into pan. Bake for 1 hour and 15 minutes, or till done. Cool cake in pan for 10 minutes before turning out.

Here, like the pound cake, is a cake that is just as good heated or toasted and that makes a divine breakfast cake. I like to serve it with tea. Freezes very well, too.

OATMEAL CAKE

CAKE

1 cup quick-cooking oats
1¼ cups boiling water
¼ pound butter, softened
1 cup sugar
1 cup brown sugar
2 eggs, beaten
1⅓ cups sifted flour
½ teaspoon salt
1 teaspoon soda
1 teaspoon nutmeg
½ teaspoon vanilla

Set oven at 375. Grease an 8-inch square pan. Soak oats in water for 20 minutes. Cream butter with sugars. Add eggs, then oatmeal. Sift together dry ingredients and add. Mix well and add vanilla. Bake for 55 minutes or till done. Remove from oven and spread topping on cake. Lower flame and place under broiler till lightly browned.

TOPPING

Mix together 4 tablespoons melter butter, ⅓ cup brown sugar, 1 can chopped cocoanut, ¼ cup quick-cooking oats and 1 tablespoon vanilla.

Here's a cake that will stay moist forever!

SURPRISE CAKE

CAKE

½ pound butter, softened
2 cups sugar
4 eggs, separated
3½ cups sifted cake flour
3½ teaspoons baking powder
¼ teaspoon salt
1 cup milk
1 teaspoon vanilla
1 teaspoon almond flavoring

Set oven at 325. Grease a 10-inch tube pan. Cream butter, add sugar, and cream till well mixed. Beat in egg yolks, one at a time. Sift dry ingredients, and add to batter alternately with milk and flavorings. Beat egg whites till stiff, and fold into batter. Bake for 1 hour and 20 minutes, or till done. While cake is baking, get to work on fillings.

FILLINGS

¾ cup milk
¼ cup sugar
2 egg yolks
2 tablespoons flour
¼ teaspoon vanilla
few drops almond flavoring

1-pound can peach halves
strawberry jam
2 squares unsweetened chocolate, melted
¼ cup sugar
3 tablespoons water
½ cup chopped nuts
1 cup heavy cream

Scald milk. Mix together sugar and yolks with fork till light and creamy. Add flour, mixing just to blend. Add milk gradually, stirring till well combined. Pour back into saucepan and cook, stirring constantly, till it reaches the boiling point. Do not boil. Add flavorings. Chill, stirring occasionally.

Drain peach halves thoroughly, then chop and mash.

When cake is done, cool completely, then split three times. Spread first layer generously with jam. Spread custard filling on second layer. Spread third layer with mashed peaches.

Make chocolate frosting. Bring sugar and water to a boil, then remove from heat and cool slightly. Mix into melted chocolate, blending well. Cool, stirring often, till thick enough to spread. Spread over top of cake and cover with chopped nuts.

Whip cream, sweeten, and flavor to taste. Spread on sides of cake, and spoon remainder into hole in center. Refrigerate.

I decided to put together a cake that had everything, and this is it. It's the end! And also the end of the book.